Beliefs

and how to

change

them...

for good!

Including the French-Burgess Belief
Gates Personal Empowerment System

BY TONY BURGESS & JULIE FRENCH

Beliefs and how to change them... for good!
Copyright ©2011 Tony Burgess and Julie French
Published in 2011 by SRA Books

SRA Books
Sue Richardson Associates
Minerva Mill Innovation Centre
Station Road
Alcester
Warwickshire B49 5ET
T: 01789 761345
www.suerichardson.co.uk

A CIP record for this book is available from the British Library.

ISBN 978-0-9567553-2-2

Designed, produced and published by Sue Richardson Associates.

Printed and bound in Great Britain by TJ International, Padstow, Cornwall

Contents ·

Acknowledgements

This book is dedicated to our wonderful children, Jez, Jenny, Molly and Sophie.

We would also like to acknowledge our wonderful clients who have been creating such positive ripples in the world using the ideas and approaches contained within these pages.

Heartfelt thanks to Sue Richardson of SRA Books for all of the professional help she has given to enable us to capture our ideas and practices most effectively in this publication.

Introduction

Thank you for
choosing this book

Thank you for choosing this book – it makes you a fellow adventurer in the exciting and stimulating world of understanding and supporting human excellence and fulfillment.

We are on a mission! To help as many people as possible to 'get out of their own way' and to enjoy living a life full of love, deep satisfaction and personal achievement - just as they were designed to. By reading this book and acting on its contents, you too can become part of that mission!

We have already shared our Belief Gates Personal Empowerment System with thousands of people and it is our intention through this book to extend the reach of the benefits of this system far beyond those that we'll ever get to meet and support face-to-face.

Enjoy experiencing the benefits for yourself and we also urge you to please share the teachings with others for good!

Thank you!

Tony Burgess and Julie French

Chapter 1

Your beliefs and how
they contribute to your
personal success

You've got to believe!

This was one of the most consistent messages that I encountered as I began my adventures in personal development, back in my mid-twenties. At the time I was hungrily reading tons of books and listening to loads of audio products on personal development, success and achievement.

Over and over again the message came at me:

'You've got to believe!'

Believe in yourself, believe in your goals, believe every moment is full of opportunities, believe there is always a way, believe in your team, in fact believe whatever you need to believe to succeed!

At the time, it readily made sense to me that *belief* could make all the difference as to whether I achieved well or not. The message was simple yet powerful. Everywhere that I sought information and tips about increasing happiness, success and achievement I was getting the clear message that 'belief' was a crucial ingredient. Of course it wasn't the *only* ingredient suggested and it *was* definitely being promoted as a crucial one.

So far, so good!

Another message that I was coming across consistently in those early days was that I should set myself some really stretching goals to allow my true potential to shine through (which really appealed to me).

Now consider a time where you may have set yourself a stretching goal. By its very stretching nature, it probably took you right up to the edge of your comfort zone and beyond. And it is when you've felt out of your comfort zone that you may have experienced 'discomfort' in one way or another. You may have done some self-doubt or anxiety or fear or uncertainty. In other words, this may have been a time where that crucial success ingredient – *believing it* – may have been diminished or missing to some degree.

I know that when I was having this 'out of comfort zone' experience myself, I really wanted to believe in myself and my goals more fully. Yet when I went back to the books, audio products and other resources,

I couldn't find the section titled 'If you ever find yourself not believing fully, here is what to do'. Instead, there was just that important powerful message 'You've got to believe'.

There was a gap in my success tool kit. The instructions on *how* to start to believe more fully while experiencing a personal 'stretch' were missing.

So I set out on a personal mission to fill that gap and find specific ways to shift any unhelpful beliefs (those that prompted self-doubt, anxiety, fear or uncertainty) and turn them into more helpful ones (those that would open the gates on my potential to achieve). Later, this also became a professional mission that carried forward into my work as a therapist, coach and trainer, along with my partner in business and in life, Julie French.

Gradually we developed a powerful, yet easy-to-apply method for making rapid and lasting belief change. Although the seeds of our ideas have germinated and grown over many years, we first presented our resulting 6-step belief change process in a brief article that we wrote in 2005. This was primarily to help our own coaching clients and it also became a powerful tool for the coaches, trainers and change facilitators that we were training. We will be sharing with you, through the pages of this book, all the details of how to apply this tried and tested 6-step belief change process to empower yourself to access and express more of your true potential in life. It will also help you to support others to be the best that they can be too.

We have now filled that important gap of how to change unhelpful beliefs into more helpful ones. We have taught our French-Burgess 6-step belief change process to thousands of people since that time and have been delighted with the really solid results that have emerged. We have used the process to support business owners, managers and leaders in organisations, speakers and performers, sportspeople, teachers, students, entrepreneurs, parents and a wide array of other people that had a sense they were made for better things and wanted more from their lives.

In addition, the many coaches, trainers and change-facilitators that we have trained since 2005 have also been using this 6-step process out there in the world with great success, resulting in a wonderful positive ripple effect emerging from our work.

We are now delighted to be personally delivering practical training with formal accreditation for professional change-facilitators to operate as practitioners of our Belief Gates Personal Empowerment System, which has at its heart our 6-step belief change process.

The potential for us collectively to make a truly significant positive difference to the world through this process is something that excites us and we are very happy for you to share our approach with everyone who can benefit. You can get proactively involved in making a positive difference through belief change and we urge you to do so!

Now, before we get into sharing the powerful belief-change process itself, let us consider for a few moments what is meant when we use the term 'belief'.

There are all kinds of fancy ways to define beliefs, coming from disciplines such as psychology, neuroscience, philosophy and theology to name just a few that have examined the topic.

In simple terms, when you have a belief, it is any thought or collection of thoughts about the world (or beyond) that you treat as 'truth' or 'fact' about the way things are.

When you consider any stream of your thinking to be falling short of 'truth' or 'fact' (for example, you consider it to be simply a possibility or a 'take' on the world or the beginnings of an opinion that you are still forming) then we could state that currently you do not fully 'believe' it. It is a thought or stream of thought, without it being a belief. Of course any of your streams of thought could potentially form into a belief in the future if persuasive or compelling evidence begins to provide support for that thought stream.

You could report your *current* beliefs (thought streams that seem true as you are thinking them or referring to them), your *old* beliefs (thought streams that you used to consider to be truth) and your desired, intended or anticipated *future* beliefs (thought streams that you would *like* to consider as truth – for example as part of your personal development journey you might have a clear desire and intention to start to believe more in your own capabilities).

Right now, your own current beliefs about yourself, the world and the things and people in that world seem very, very real, don't they?

This is experienced by most people. People (unsurprisingly) believe their own beliefs. It *seems* to most individuals that their beliefs are a direct and accurate representation of the way the world is. Your own beliefs *seem* so true (to you). It *seems* (to you) like your beliefs are fact. It *seems* (to you) like you have *the* right answer or *the* right perspective or *the* right solution when you believe in it.

In fact, beliefs are far from a direct representation of reality. Any belief you hold is actually a heavily filtered, biased version (among many possible versions) of the way things are in the world (and beyond). So even though it *seems* so real, any belief that you hold is largely made up!

Even when people are seemingly in agreement about something being true, they all have their own subtle versions of that so-called 'truth' represented (re-presented) inside their minds.

All of your perceptions, all of your thoughts, all of your beliefs are full of *distortions* and *generalisations*. Also lots of information is *deleted* by your mind when your thought, idea, perception or belief is occurring.

Your mind has evolved to delete most information from your moment-by-moment awareness to help you to function and perform. It is trying to make the vast array of sensory signals bombarding you every second more manageable so that you can more readily make sense of what is happening (and then potentially act on it). So your mind lets some information into awareness and misses other information out.

Your mind also gives meanings to incoming information and makes assumptions about what has caused things and also tries to make information fit with existing mental structures.

Your mind also tries to spot patterns and similarities and differences between what is being sensed now and what has previously been experienced.

In many ways this messing with the raw data helps us all function as human beings. Imagine if you or I had to start from scratch to learn what a door is for and how to operate it each and every time we encountered one. We'd probably struggle to even travel around our own home efficiently. Also, imagine if we had to consciously process and attend to every bit of information hitting our senses every second. I'm sure you will agree that we would be unlikely to be able to truly focus on what is most relevant and important for us.

Our minds filter (delete, distort and generalise) new information automatically according to our state, role, past experiences, expectations, sense of purpose and context, personal rules, values and current beliefs (to name but a few).

So why is it going to be important for you to be able to work with beliefs? As previously mentioned, your current beliefs are powerful filters on new incoming information that forms your next waves of thought and perception. Your mind likes to filter information so that it fits with your existing beliefs. That means that you'll tend to get more of what you are looking for. You'll get more of what you believe in.

Your beliefs are also powerful influencers on your behaviour and emotional responses. We are motivated to behave and respond in ways that are consistent with our beliefs and we tend to experience discomfort when we're acting in ways that are contrary to our beliefs.

"So what?" you may be wondering.

Well your beliefs can be powerfully *helpful* to you if they are stimulating future thoughts, perceptions and behaviours that serve you in attaining your desired outcomes, experiences and goals. And I'm sure you will also be able to recognise that some of your beliefs may have been debilitatingly *unhelpful* to you when they've been stimulating thoughts, perceptions and behaviours that were misaligned with or were *getting in the way* of the attainment of your desired outcomes, experiences and goals.

The beliefs you hold, affect what happens next. *They affect results!*

Beliefs can determine whether the gates on your inner resourcefulness are open or closed. They can affect whether your greatness shines through or not. This can be the difference between 'can' and 'can't', success or absence of success, possible and impossible, contentment and discontentment, healthy and unhealthy, win or lose.

You tend to notice more of what you believe in. You let in more of what you believe in. You expect more of what you believe in. You respond as if the world is how you believe it to be. And when your actions and activities are aligned with your beliefs, you tend to get results that are consistent with whatever you believe in.

So if you want different results, outcomes, or experiences in your life, you would do well to work on changing some of your beliefs first.

Taking such an inside-out approach to your personal development will mean any positive change in your behaviour will be more wholeheartedly adopted and the results will tend to have more stickability and longevity for you.

Chapter 2

Thinking differently
about beliefs

I'm going to encourage you to start to think about your beliefs in new ways.

Most people judge beliefs (their own and others) as being 'correct' or 'incorrect'/'right' or 'wrong'/'valid' or 'invalid' – usually considering their own as being correct/right/valid and other people's (if different to theirs) to be incorrect/wrong/invalid to some extent (even if they do not openly object to those 'wrong' beliefs).

Millions of people, across the whole of human history, have engaged in interpersonal conflict to defend their beliefs. From arguments with neighbours, peers, colleagues, partners, family and friends through to full-scale wars! Actions and responses in the name of defending the 'truth' of beliefs have contributed to a great deal of misery across history and continue to do so right through to today.

Even when arguments or wars have been won and lost, the 'truth' that was being fought over has often remained unsettled. Resentment may linger and people may only temporarily 'fall into line' begrudgingly unless a genuine belief shift has happened.

To help you to make your beliefs into powerful tools that can work for you day by day, to help you to achieve your desired goals, outcomes and experiences, I am going to suggest another way of considering them beyond the usual 'correct/incorrect', 'right/wrong', or 'valid/invalid' categories.

The alternative evaluation method I am going to propose will also help you support others to attain their desired goals, outcomes and experiences. It will also help you facilitate the achievement of collective (e.g. team) goals, outcomes and experiences.

The new approach I am suggesting is that you set aside any consideration of whether a belief is true or false and instead ask the question, "Is this belief helpful or unhelpful, given what I (or 'you' or 'we') want to achieve/experience?"

- Is the belief *smoothing the way* to progress or *getting in the way* of progress?

- Is it *opening the gates* or *shutting the gates* on your resourcefulness?

- Is it helping you to *thrive* or is it keeping you *stuck* or moving you further *away* from your desired outcomes?

By suspending the matter of 'truth' (which is forever debatable anyway) we can instead focus on what is working/not working. This shift from evaluating our beliefs as true or false to evaluating them as helpful or unhelpful can be a powerfully positive step for us when we wish to attain different results in life, whether it be in sport, business, personal development, therapy or any other area of focus.

This new way of thinking about our beliefs allows a pragmatic approach. If a belief is 'working' for you then you can learn to reinforce it, strengthen it, do more of it, maybe even apply it to other areas of your life where it could also work (modeling your own excellence). If however any belief is not working for you (getting in the way of progress) then you can learn to challenge and/or replace it with one that will work better for you in terms of allowing, easing or accelerating progress.

A common objection to this suggested approach to evaluating beliefs as helpful/unhelpful rather than true/false goes something like this...

> *"How on earth can I drop a belief just because it is unhelpful? I have had this belief for years, most of my life in fact! I can't just swap beliefs when I feel like it, just because it could get me better results! Beliefs just don't change that easily"*

...which is, of course, in itself... a belief (and if it is getting in the way of you making progress, it may be the first one that you work on changing!).

My experience as a human being, therapist, coach and trainer has provided me with many opportunities to experience and demonstrate over and over again just how quickly and easily a person can in fact drop an unhelpful belief and replace it with a more helpful one, given the right tools (irrespective of how long they have held onto the unhelpful one previously). And I continue to be a successful catalyst for such positive change, in part due to my strong *belief* that rapid and lasting belief change is very possible and can be easy.

Check out your own current beliefs about the *possibility/impossibility* or *ease/difficulty* of making rapid and lasting belief changes. And now ask yourself: "Are those beliefs helpful or unhelpful?" given that some of your desired goals or outcomes could really benefit from such rapid and lasting belief change.

If you have noticed that any of your beliefs about 'belief change' are potentially 'unhelpful' then please pause for a moment and make a commitment to yourself to replace them as you work through later chapters. I urge you - Make that commitment to yourself right now!

Adopting helpful beliefs: Personal empowerment or delusion?

An interesting debate (which by the way has 'proof' available for all sides, meaning there are several potential 'truths') is whether we are truly empowering ourselves and others when we choose to adopt more helpful beliefs or whether we are just encouraging delusion and false hope.

It is a controversy that we could keep debating for centuries without resolving it and I am going to consider it briefly here.

We have all heard the true stories about people who've achieved outstanding results because they kept on believing in themselves and their goal even when all around them were convinced it was just 'pie in the sky' and were telling them it wasn't going to happen.

There are many famous writers, performers, film stars, inventors and entrepreneurs who have previously been rejected over and over again; or they were told they were not good enough or strong enough or capable enough; or they hit broke before they finally made it. These are all living testament to the power of self-belief fuelling persistence. Some people that you may want to look into include: J K Rowling, James Dyson, Stephen King, The Beatles, Sylvester Stallone and Eddie Izzard.

Equally there are many true stories about people finding themselves in extreme circumstances where their survival hangs in the balance. Despite seemingly overwhelming odds against them, such stories tell how spirited individuals have managed to continue to believe they could make it, driving them to take determined action and ultimately helping them to survive their ordeals. Some well-documented modern true stories that demonstrate an important role for the power of belief in aiding survival include: *Alive* by Piers Paul Read (Mandarin, 1993), *Touching the Void* by Joe Simpson (Vintage, 1998), *Lost in the Jungle* by Yossi Ghinsberg (Summersdale, 2008) and *66 Days Adrift* by William Butler (McGraw Hill, 2005).

Of course there are many accounts that can be told of people who do not hit the headlines or get their story told in a book, who in their day to day lives are living examples of how beliefs can have powerful positive impact, for example in coping with illness, poverty, hardship, oppression, imprisonment, violence and bereavement. I encourage you to start to notice how some people seem to keep positive, strong, optimistic and relatively fulfilled despite major challenges in their lives. I also encourage you to notice how some other people seem to easily find negative angles on situations and much to moan about despite their seemingly easy lives. Get curious about how different the beliefs are from one extreme to the other and what affect these different beliefs can have on people's well-being.

So there are plenty of real-life indicators that beliefs can potentially make a truly positive difference to achievement and success (and survival) and yet there are also some situations that prompt many people to wonder whether 'self-belief' equates to unhelpful 'self-delusion'.

Mainstream TV provides us with a large selection of high profile talent competitions filled with many clear examples showing what is at the heart of this controversy.

I am sure you have seen the kind of scene I am referring to - where a contestant strides cockily onto stage ready to face a panel of influential judges and an expectant audience. There's a pause.

They look confident.

Then they say a few words about their intention to become the next big star.

They certainly seem as if they believe in themselves.

Maybe this is going to be one of those rare magic moments where a star is indeed born, live on television?

And then they begin to sing…..

The sound is horrible!

The performance is a disaster.

The judges are looking in disbelief. They are exasperated.

The audience is booing and shouting for the contestant to get off the stage.

The music stops.

The contestant looks defiant …and then speaks out loudly in anger:

"Who do you think you are?"

"You obviously don't know talent when you hear it."

"You'll be sorry you didn't sign me up while you had your chance!"

They storm off stage shouting "This is your loss! I'm the best singer this competition has ever seen", as the audience roars with laughter and mocks them as they exit the competition.

And they really believe their own words!

Despite all the evidence that is staring them in the face – they truly believe that they can sing extraordinarily well and that the judges and the audience had missed the 'truth' of their talent.

Over the coming years they'll continue doing exactly what they've been doing before and await someone to notice how great their singing 'talent' really is.

Surely this scenario provides proof that people can believe in themselves all they want and it won't positively affect their actual performance?

Well maybe there is more to it than that.

We certainly have plenty of compelling real-life stories that suggest that empowering beliefs can make a positive and useful difference to what people achieve. And we also have clear examples where it seems like self-belief equates to outlandish self-delusion.

From this we can conclude that…

Holding positive empowering beliefs clearly works!

And…

Holding positive empowering beliefs clearly doesn't work!

It does when it does and it doesn't when it doesn't.

Let's consider this a little further!

'Believing' is certainly one crucial ingredient for success … and as I said earlier, it is not the only one!

Other ingredients that you could incorporate nicely with 'believing', so that you massively increase the odds that this will work for you (or any person you are helping) are:

- To 'model' what has worked for others to attain the same kind of outcome (in other words learn from others who have already made it happen!).

- To listen to solution-focused advice of supportive others who have already achieved what you intend to achieve (or have at least achieved stretching goals successfully).

- To pay attention to whether what you are currently doing is working or not and being willing to tweak and change activity (inside and out) based on what you notice.

- To commit to taking appropriate (sometimes massive) action aligned with the direction of your goal, outcome or desired experience.

So let's go back for a moment to the person who was such a laughing stock in the singing talent show.

The current feedback from experts and decision makers in the music business tells them that their singing is presently way below standard. The audience that they intended and expected to please is giving obvious and loud feedback about how way-off-target their singing really is.

The very fact that they are voted out of the competition in the first round is confirming that their current standard is far from hitting the spot.

In such a situation, sticking to a positive belief 'At my current performance level I am singing beautifully and at a level that will make me a star' would be unhelpful. It would tend to keep leading to the same undesirable results. It would be unhelpful 'delusion'. Believing it alone is not enough in this scenario.

If that person instead held on to a belief that 'I have the capacity to improve my singing and performance with help and dedication and commitment' and then they acted on that belief and on the advice of supportive achievers in the field and they 'modeled' the success behaviours that helped others to turn things around dramatically and they made those activities an absolute priority and a key focus for themselves each and every day.... then that is where the *seeming impossible* can start to become possible. They could potentially massively turn things around and surprise everyone. Self-belief could play a crucial role during a journey like this that seemed 'against the odds' and the other ingredients would be needed too in order to really turn things around.

Now let us also briefly consider the following argument which I have heard voiced often:

What if after all of that effort they still didn't get their desired outcome?

Well my answer would be this: They would have a) made an empowering choice to have given themselves the very best chance of achieving their outcome and b) they would have learned and achieved and developed at a level far higher than if they had not embarked on the mission (e.g. if they had held back because of self-doubt or fear or anxiety) and all of that learning and development is transferable into new personal and professional journeys.

Remember that often when people are doing self-doubt, fear and anxiety about their own potential and their own capabilities, they are actually deluding themselves in unhelpful ways. And that unhelpful delusion affects results!

Only time will tell whether any individual 'believing it' actually gets their desired goal, outcome or experience on any particular success journey. On those occasions where any desired result does not occur, it is unlikely to have been because they believed it. It is more likely to be due to them being closed to noticing what is working or being closed to taking necessary action or unwilling to tweak behaviours.

Of course, my very *belief* (which could be argued against) that 'having helpful beliefs, will better pave the way for goal achievement' does in itself help prompt a positive self-fulfilling prophecy for me and the people that I support. And in my view, that is a very good practical reason for keeping that belief.

As I have indicated before, if you're intending to make belief change a key process to help you get better results, I would encourage you to adopt a belief...that 'belief change works!'

Chapter 3

Some of the most
powerful kinds of belief

Much of your 'inner stuff' (the activity that goes on in your mind and your emotional responses) is interconnected in one way or another with your beliefs.

Some kinds of belief will have a particularly powerful impact on such mental processing and emotions (and in turn, on your behaviour).

Here are the beliefs that my experience tells me are the most powerful:

1. Your beliefs about your purpose in life.
2. Your beliefs about who you are – your sense of identity
3. Your beliefs about what is really important – your values

Your beliefs about your purpose in life

Beliefs about purpose can include a sense of 'calling' or 'vocation', or can sometimes connect to serving God or to serving a cause or humanity in some way.

Many people can go through much of their life with no real strong sense of purpose (although they are likely to have had glimpses from time to time, when they are really 'in their flow' during an activity or experience). Some people seem to be totally living 'on purpose' most of the time. Others are soul-searching and on a personal journey to finding their sense of purpose.

What is your current level of purposefulness?

To what degree have you got a clear sense of what your life is ultimately about and what you are here for?

Whatever your current answers are to such questions, we can all relate to what it is like to meet someone when they are truly connected to their sense of purpose. It is like they are unstoppable. The clarity of their beliefs about why they are here and what their purpose is in life seems to open the gates on their massive resourcefulness and things seem to be really happening as a result.

Your sense of purpose will have a massive influence on your level of activity, choice of behaviours, what you focus on, how you prioritise, what you accept and reject and how you live and connect with other people moment by moment.

If you set any goal in a way that seems counter to your beliefs about your purpose, it is highly unlikely that you will connect to it fully and achieve it at the highest level. Whereas any goal that seems highly relevant to your beliefs about your purpose will be given plenty of resources and focus and attention, which will positively influence the odds of you achieving your outcome at the highest level.

Two key lessons emerge from this.

First, developing powerful beliefs about purpose can really help make things happen and helping someone to explore this can be a real gift to them. Second, making sure that all goals are aligned with beliefs about purpose (or vice versa) is pretty crucial for maximising progress.

Your beliefs about who you are – your sense of identity:

When you hold a belief about who you are as a person (usually such beliefs include thoughts that begin 'I am….') it tends to give the associated behaviours, assumptions, experiences and emotions some longevity and stickability.

If you believe that something is true about *the very essence of who you are*, then psychologically you will respond as if this quality or attribute is going to stick around. If instead you believe that something is true only at the level of your experience or your behaviour, then psychologically it has a more *transient* or *temporary* quality about it.

So a belief: 'I *am* stupid' will tend to encourage a sense that 'this is here to stay' (just as 'I am tall' would tend to be considered permanent) whereas a belief: '*What I just did* in that moment was stupid' tends to be considered as more transient, because it is over and done with and it was only behaviour anyway.

The powerful psychological effect of 'I am…' self-beliefs can really serve you well, so long as those self-beliefs are useful ones (in relation to your goals and desired experiences and outcomes).

So holding a self belief such as 'I am a highly capable and lovable person', would be highly likely to serve you in relation to most of your desired goals, experiences and outcomes. Because it has the 'I am....' structure to it, psychologically it is treated as something that has permanence and can be drawn on over and over again and can show up in behaviours and experiences over and over again. In contrast, if you had mentally played down any evidence of capability and lovable-ness by referring to it *only* at the level of experience or behaviour (such as 'I did a good job just then' or 'I felt loved in that moment'), there is a danger that psychologically your system would treat it as transient or as just an exception, particularly if there was also a powerful self-belief in place that 'I *am* a person with low capability and low potential to achieve'.

The identity level beliefs ('I am...') will hold considerable power and influence over your present and future responses and experiences.

With this in mind, the more that you can develop really helpful and empowering self-beliefs, the more you are likely to stimulate and give longevity to helpful behaviours and experiences.

Examples of self-beliefs that may serve you well in relation to many of your goals and desired outcomes could include....

- 'I am capable'
- 'I am a great learner'
- 'I am flexible'
- 'I am resourceful'
- 'I am of value'

Whereas examples of beliefs that may have got in the way of progress relating to desired goals and outcomes could include....

- 'I am average'
- 'I am a poor learner'

- 'I am no good'
- 'I am useless'
- 'I am not good enough'
- 'I am of no value'

Check out your own self-beliefs. Get a piece of paper and put 'I am....' at the top of the page. Then write down intuitively as many endings to the sentence as possible in three or four minutes.

Then take a good look and ask yourself:

'Given what I want to achieve and experience in my life, how well are these self-beliefs serving me?'

Pick out those that seem to be supporting you and the journey to your desired outcomes and put a tick next to them. Take every opportunity to remind yourself of these and reinforce them.

Any self-beliefs that seem to be getting in the way of you getting what you want in terms of goals and experiences in life can be 'flagged up' as ones to change using the 6-step belief change process that we will introduce in later chapters.

You can help others by communicating useful things that you notice about them at the level of their identity, using 'You are...' phrases.

It is important to make this a congruent and authentic communication (people are generally pretty good at spotting incongruence). First, train yourself to genuinely look out for and spot admirable qualities in people (practise it), then commit to communicating what you notice by referring to it at the identity level ('You are...').

For example, someone does something helpful. You have choices about how you respond to that. And how you choose to respond will have a particular psychological effect on the other person and will also affect the likelihood of such helpfulness occurring again!

So you could just notice it and say nothing (which is in fact very common when people are mainly noticing and putting their attention on *un*helpful behaviours).

Or you could notice it and say 'What you just did was really helpful because… X, Y and Z' which could be useful for the person to hear as an acknowledgement (if communicated authentically) and may sometimes be minimised (played down) to some extent as being 'transient' or only an 'exception' in their behavioural repertoire.

Or you could notice it and say '*You are* really helpful. For example, what you did just then really helped because….X, Y and Z'. This would tend to communicate that you are seeing a permanence to that quality (helpful) in the person because you are seeing it as *who they are* rather than only as *what they did* on this occasion.

Equally, when you notice anything a person has done or experienced that has been getting in the way of their progress, communicate about it (when appropriate) in a way that suggests it to be *transient* and *fluid* and *changeable* – at the level of behavior and experience rather than identity.

An example would be as follows:

You notice something that is not working for a person (in relation to their goals or desired outcomes or perhaps in relation to collective goals or outcomes). Again, you have choices about how you respond to what you have noticed.

You could simply notice it and say nothing. This can sometimes be helpful if it is fairly insignificant. Simply acknowledging the helpful things you notice can be a really helpful approach in many circumstances.

Or you could notice and comment about it at the identity level by saying 'You are so unhelpful! You are hopeless! You are a nightmare to work with' (okay this is an extreme response and you get the point about the 'You are…' structure to the communication). There is a danger that this could either lead to a defensive response from the person because you are threatening their very identity, or it may lead to the person psychologically assigning some stickability to the unhelpfulness if they *accept* your criticism. In effect they would internalise it as 'This is who I am. I can't change who I am. This is going to show up again and again. I might as well get used to it'.

Another choice you could make would be to respond about the unhelpfulness at the behavioural or experiential level (separating it from their identity). You could say 'What you just did really wasn't working because X, Y and Z. As a highly capable person, I know that you can find ways to make this more helpful in future, I would like to hear your ideas about that'. This communicates that some *behaviour* was unhelpful. Psychologically, behaviour is separate from someone's identity and behaviour is perceived as more changeable than identity, so there is perceived room for improvement. This kind of communication is less threatening because it is referring to behaviour rather than the person. Also, notice that the second part of the response was referring to the person's identity ('As a highly capable *person*...') and did so in a helpful way relating to the helpful quality of 'being capable'. The final sentence 'I would like to hear your ideas about that' communicates that you can see the potential in the person for positively changing their behaviours and that they can be the source of the solutions (again conveying your conviction in them as a valued and capable person).

To sum up:

- Link things to identity that are 'working' – help build these into the self-beliefs of yourself and others by using 'I am...' and 'You are...' communications as appropriate. This frames 'what is working' as potentially permanent and encourages it to show up more often.

- Separate those things that are 'not working' from identity – help to keep them out of the self-beliefs of yourself and others by using behavioural and experiential communications such as 'What you (or I) just did....' or 'What you (or I) just experienced....' This frames it as being more 'transient' and changeable.

Your beliefs about what is really important – your values:

Something that you believe is important will have more impact on your behaviour than something that you believe to be unimportant.

That is a simple point and yet a powerful one.

Sometimes people ask themselves (or others) to do things that are against their values and this is a sure way to get resistance or rebellion or only half-hearted engagement.

Many people have surprisingly little conscious awareness of the core values of those who they care about and wish to influence, support, help, live with or work with.

Some people also have given little thought as to their own core values and how they might align or misalign with current goals.

Demanding of yourself that you do something that you perceive to be against one or more of your core values is a sure way to trigger self-sabotage or discontentment. Demanding of others any activities that go against the grain of their core values is a sure way to either limit progress or trigger resentment in others.

On the other hand, aligning goals and your communications about goals (including your inner communications with yourself) with core values is a recipe for engagement and progress.

When you want to influence others to make a change, it is likely that you will do well to communicate in different ways with different people, according to their most powerful values. You will need to 'sell' an idea in relation to what is believed to be particularly important by any specific individual.

For example, let's imagine that a woman called Karen has a life partner called Paul and Karen wishes to encourage Paul to spend more undistracted time with her.

Karen would do well to 'sell' the idea in her communications in a way that is aligned with Paul's core values. So if Paul believed strongly that it is extremely important 'to maximise harmony' then Karen might 'sell' the desired outcome to Paul in terms of how spending more undistracted time together will improve harmony in their relationship (or how not doing so could compromise harmony).

If on the other hand Paul really values health as a top priority then Karen might 'sell' the idea in terms of the benefits to health that will come from spending more undistracted time together (or potential damage to health if this did not happen).

Or if Paul put a really high value on having fun in life, Karen could emphasise the possibilities for fun.

And if Paul believes it is hugely important in life to be making plenty of money, Karen could 'sell' the benefits of spending more undistracted time together in terms of feeling refreshed and becoming even more ready for making lots of money. And so on.

I encourage you to capture as much as you can about your own values and the values of those whom you wish to influence positively.

This gives you the awareness that allows you to tailor your communications (with self and others) to best stimulate 'buy-in' to taking helpful actions that are aligned with goals and desired outcomes.

A simple way for you to begin to capture your own values would be as follows:

Imagine that you could be a 'fly on the wall' in the company of various key people in your work and personal life. Ask yourself what you would **love** to overhear them saying about you behind your back? This will allow you to get a sense of what is really important to you in the different areas of your life.

From the sentences that you might love to overhear them saying it is often only a small step to translating them into values. For example, if I were to notice that I would love my colleagues to say behind my back that 'He makes a really positive difference to everyone that he meets' then I might extract from that the value of 'making a positive difference'.

Once you have a list of values (things that you believe to be important) in a range of different contexts or areas of your life, I suggest that you put them in some kind of priority order to understand which are the most important ones (which will be the biggest influencers on behaviour and experience). To do this, ask yourself questions such as… 'If I could only keep 10 of these values and had to ditch the rest, which 10 would I keep?' Then you can lower the number further by asking 'Out of these 10 values, if I could only keep 5, which would they be?' and so on.

Ask yourself how you might find out more about the values of other people in your life. You might adopt playful approaches (as in the example given for checking out your own values) or more conversational approaches (such as to regularly ask questions such as 'What is it that you find most important about that?'). You could also use more formal methods such as giving people a large number of values written on a page and asking them to rank them in priority order.

Get inventive and take action to find out more about what individuals (whom you wish to influence in positive ways) believe to be most important in life.

Chapter 4

Step 1 in our 6-Step Belief Change Process: Knowing the desired outcome

You can only decide on the usefulness or helpfulness of any belief or set of beliefs when you have an answer to the question 'in relation to what desired outcome?'

This may seem a simple and straightforward point and yet so often I work with clients where they arrive wishing to make a positive change and yet their head is mainly filled with all of the things that they *do not* want or the things they've had enough of, rather than where they want to progress to.

Although we can acknowledge that noticing what we've had enough of can be a motivator to kick-start a decision to make a change, it's also important to recognise that, for most people, dwelling on what they don't want (what they wish to avoid or what they are sick and tired of) can also sometimes trigger less resourceful states such as a sense of hopelessness, overwhelm or powerlessness and sometimes this gets people feeling stuck.

Another downside to mainly focusing on what we don't want would be that our system would have no clear positive reference for where to go next.

So for us to move forward successfully it is also very important to begin to face in a more useful direction by proactively answering the question 'so what exactly is it that I *do* want?'

Motorcycling provides a great metaphorical example of how we will tend to get more of what we are focusing on. I remember when I was first learning how to ride a motorcycle about 12 years ago. I know that I was feeling way out of my comfort zone and I admit that there were times where I was definitely 'getting in my own way'. I caught myself focusing on lots of things that I wanted to avoid – places that I did *not* want my motorcycle to steer towards (for example, I would be paying attention to *not* hitting the kerb, *not* hitting parked cars, *not* steering towards damaged areas of the road surface, etc). And to my horror, my motorcycle began steering me towards those very things I was focusing on!

It was like the motorcycle knew!

And of course in a way it did, because my mind was controlling my body which controlled the equipment!

This was a very quick and scary lesson. I rapidly realised that I needed to start focusing on where I *did* want my motorcycle to take me. And immediately, the direction of the motorcycle corrected! It took me wherever I focused my attention.

I am told that a similar effect can be noticed when skiing or horse riding and I am sure you can think of your own examples that you have experienced too.

So focusing on what you *do* want will begin to send more helpful instructions to every cell of your body as to where to steer you and your life next. And helping others to do the same will be a great gift for you to give them.

A good friend of ours, Steve Halls (www.stevehalls.co.uk) has a wonderful way of making this point about the importance of focusing on where you *do* want to steer things. He likens our human system to a search engine. It 'searches' according to key words. For example, if you put in a search engine 'no Spanish holiday villas' you would get thousands or even millions of listings that were about Spanish holiday villas even though you had indicated that you wanted none of them with the word 'no'. The search engine responded mainly to the key words and concepts and fetched accordingly. Whether you wanted those results or wanted to avoid those results is given little relevance – it fetches anyway!

In a similar vein, if my friend or colleague was circulating thoughts like 'I don't want stress', 'no more being broke', 'I've had enough of messing up' they would have been inadvertently 'priming' their whole system to notice, search for and fetch more of the very outcomes that they did not want.

The human system, waiting eagerly to receive and follow instructions will simply go with the key concepts that are being circulated and focused on.

Train yourself, when goal setting and also during moment to moment thinking to focus on where you *do* want to steer things, on what you *do* want your system to be primed to fetch.

Also help others to increase their awareness of how they are phrasing their desired goals and outcomes and how they talk about and think about them moment by moment. Encourage them to point their thoughts and their language in the direction of what they do want as their outcomes.

Exercise

Decide on something that you do currently want and write it down.

Go ahead, do it now – I urge you!

It could be one of those recurring resolutions or a goal where you may have been feeling stuck or finding progress slow or hard work.

We are going to use this goal as the focal point when applying all of the remaining steps.

Chapter 5

Step 2 in our 6-Step
Belief Change Process:
The beliefs audit

Now that you know what you *do* want, you are in position to judge whether a belief (or set of beliefs) is helpful or unhelpful *in relation to* what you do want!

It is so important that you have a particular outcome in mind when you make that judgement because the same belief could be 'helpful' to you achieving one outcome and yet 'unhelpful' or getting in the way of you achieving another.

To illustrate this, let's take the belief 'This is difficult'.

I may find the belief to be helpful and even a driver for action if I was excitedly looking for a really stretching challenge in my leisure time, such as committing to run a marathon to crank up my fitness. If taking on a tough challenge was a clear goal for me, I may be in danger of losing some interest before I even got started if I held the belief that 'This is really easy'.

I may however find the very same belief ('This is difficult') to be unhelpful in another situation where perhaps I was already experiencing some self-doubts about a new task or a new situation.

Here an alternative belief could be really useful, to help me to re-open the gates on my resourcefulness so I can thrive. This is where applying the six steps to adopt more helpful beliefs would make a lot of good sense.

So the real question is this: 'Is this belief, in this scenario, with this outcome in mind, serving me or getting in the way?'

Be careful – when supporting others in checking out their beliefs, let *them* decide whether any specific belief is helpful or unhelpful. What may be helpful for you, may not necessarily be helpful to someone else.

For example, for one person, a belief that 'My friends do not believe I can make this happen' might be unhelpful and demoralising and for another person it may be helpful because it spurs them on to show their friends that they can in fact make it happen.

So when it is *your* beliefs that you are assessing for usefulness, *you* be the judge. When it is another person's beliefs, let *them* be the judge!

Auditing your beliefs:

It's time to start to get curious about what's going on in there! On a blank sheet of paper draw a line down the middle so that you have two columns. At the top of one column write 'unhelpful beliefs' and at the top of the other column write 'helpful beliefs'.

Now, thinking of your goal or desired outcome, allow your beliefs and assumptions (those things that you think you know) in relation to that goal or outcome to bubble up to the surface of your awareness. They may be beliefs about how possible your goal is to achieve, how easy or difficult it is, how capable you believe you are. They may be beliefs about other people, beliefs about the timescale required to achieve, or beliefs about what things mean. Write as many as you can, sorting them into columns, as they come to mind, according to whether they are 'helpful' or 'unhelpful'. Then looking at the 'unhelpful' column, circle the belief that you feel is the most significantly unhelpful or 'in the way' in relation to you achieving the particular outcome or goal that you have in mind.

Whatever belief you have circled will be the belief that we are going to be changing in the following four remaining steps of the belief change process. The reason we go with the seemingly most significantly unhelpful one first is that as we change it, other unhelpful beliefs in the list will often shift too.

You can always repeat the remaining four steps with any other beliefs that have fallen into the 'unhelpful' column and you might as well start by making the most powerful belief shift first.

Chapter 6

Step 3 in our 6-Step
Belief Change Process:
The power of 'what-iffing'

As human beings, we have very many skills and one of the human skills that is both widespread and powerful is the skill that we call 'what-iffing' (or asking 'what if?' questions.) Asking 'what if?' questions can have powerful impact for sure and the only problem is that many of the 'what if?' questions that people tend to ask themselves and each other are actually pretty unhelpful.

For example we may have asked questions like 'What if it goes horribly wrong?', 'What if they don't like me?', 'What if I fall flat on my face?' These kinds of questions would most likely have got in the way of us achieving our desired outcomes and goals. We've been putting the wrong search words into the search engine!

Of course an exception would be if we purposefully asked such disaster-oriented 'what if?' questions as part of a project management process, to help stimulate great *solutions* to potential difficulties, up front. This can be useful if we remain in a solution-focused mode. I feel compelled to report that my experience of working with project managers is that once they step out of role and go home to their families and to their personal goals, they are just as likely as anyone else to start to ask disaster-oriented questions in a way that limits their progress rather than supports it.

When in the past you or I have asked ourselves unhelpful 'what if?' questions, (for example where the questions have invoked self-doubt or anxiety), most often it would have closed the gates on our resourcefulness and had us feeling disempowered or stuck. Clearly this would have got in the way.

What is delightful to notice at this point is that the very power of 'what-iffing' that might have previously kept us stuck can also be channelled in a positive direction to open up the gates on our resourcefulness and free us to move forward effectively.

In step 3 of our 6-step belief change process, the idea is for you to come up with a list of positive 'what if?' questions that will counter your original unhelpful belief (that you circled in the unhelpful column of the beliefs audit) and begin to open the gates on your resourcefulness. When you deliberately ask these useful 'what if?' questions of yourself, putting a helpful tonality to your thinking voice (eg a tonality of excited curiosity), you will notice your whole system starting to be tantalisingly tempted towards the new possibilities. This is where your old belief can start to shake a little as your mind is beginning to be attracted towards alternative perspectives. Your thinking begins to steer your whole system in a more helpful direction. The questions help you to begin to uncover new possibilities. And even as you ask these positive 'what if?' questions to yourself, you may notice a part of you is beginning to acknowledge some of the elements that could be true for you (could be *believed*).

Exercise: Begin your helpful 'What-iffing'

Working with the one significant unhelpful belief that you have circled (in the audit), now come up with as many positive alternative questions as you can. For example, if your unhelpful belief was 'this is going to be difficult' you might start to come up with positive alternative questions such as 'What if it's easier than I think? 'What if it's just the first step that appears that way and the next steps will get easier and easier? 'What if I've got all the resourcefulness I need in order to start to make this easy?' 'What if it is just like another time when something seemed difficult and turned out to be easier than I had expected?', 'What if I just need to get out of my own way?' and so on…

Once you have finished writing as many as you can, read them over and over in your mind with that excited curiosity in the tonality of your thinking voice and notice which 'what ifs?' are most significantly and powerfully attractive and helpful as alternatives to the original unhelpful belief.

Which one stands out above all others, where you think 'Wow, if I truly believed that to be the case, right to my core, it would definitely help me make progress'? Put a circle around that one as it is the one we will take forward to step 4.

(Bear in mind that you can of course take all of the useful 'what if' questions through to the remaining steps when you find it helpful to do so. And as before I am encouraging you to start by taking forward the one that will make the biggest positive difference).

Chapter 7

Step 4 in our 6-Step
Belief Change Process:
The debate

Having applied the first three steps of the process, you will have already begun to notice your beliefs shifting positively.

Step 4 is designed to build up some evidence to support the growth of the green shoot of a belief contained in your most helpful 'what if?' question. This will satisfy any of your conscious logical questioning faculties and will continue the process of turning a tantalising possibility into a personal truth (a belief).

Importantly, step 4 – the debate – provides opportunities for you to add supporting 'legs' to your newly forming belief.

As a participant in a classroom debate you would very likely be given a random subject to argue for or against and even though you may not (yet) believe in the position, it would be your job to come up with as many arguments as you could to convince the judges that your prescribed standpoint is the most believable. Solid evidence and convincing argument can be found in the most outlandish of positions. (After all, when you think about it, in the past, we would have accepted and acted on plenty of unhelpful beliefs that may now seem ridiculous! And we'd have easily added 'legs' to them and probably defended them for years.)

Exercise: Start the debate!

Take your most appealing and powerful positive 'what if'? question and write it at the top of a piece of paper. Now cross out the words 'what if' at the beginning of the question (and also remove the question mark) and now add the word 'because....' at the end.

For example, the question ...

'What if it's easier than I think?' ... would become...

'It's easier than I think because....'

Now, give yourself full permission to go on a mission to

complete the statement with as much supporting evidence as you can generate or bring to mind.

Allow yourself to say the arguments out loud whilst deliberately using the tonality of conviction and certainty as though your life depended on convincing people that the position is true (your goal may well depend on it after all!)

The more you engage in full-on 'selling' of the position, the more your physiology and your mind will be accepting the possibility as a feasible one. Repetition and speaking out loud will build the 'case' for the new position, with increasing conviction in the tonality and giving yourself full permission to add in extra evidence as it begins to occur to you.

So now your new, more helpful perspective is starting to genuinely stack up, to become a more solid belief (rather than an interesting tempting possibility).

On many occasions when we have helped people to change their beliefs, at the end of step 4, the work is now done. The belief change is already complete and authentic. And we have two more steps for you to really embed this new belief at an even more powerful level.

Chapter 8

Step 5 in our 6-Step
Belief Change Process:
Mental rehearsal

Now that your case for your new 'truth' is beginning to become more believable, we need to start to literally programme it in by turning the evidence into an experience. Many top sports people disclose that they frequently (and sometimes continuously) use mental rehearsal/visualisation of themselves winning as a key psychological process in preparation for top level achievement. A few years ago my partner Julie interviewed Olympic gold medallist Sally Gunnell on stage to discover what degree of mental preparation she had done in the lead up to the 1992 Barcelona Olympics. She told us that, after she had not achieved what she sensed she was capable of achieving in the previous Olympics, she knew she had to do something different. She decided to include much more mental preparation in her training schedule and for over 12 months before the 1992 Olympics, each and every day, several times a day she visualised herself winning her race. That kind of preparation takes real commitment and of course it also gets results because you are filling your mind, over and over again, with the experiences that you intend to create for yourself. This intense programming activity adds more supporting legs to the enticing possibilities and turns them into even more solid beliefs!

We often use the term 'mental rehearsal' rather than 'visualisation' only because the degree to which people represent the world in thought pictures or thought movies will vary to some extent and so playing the scenario through in your head may or may not have a strong and clear visual element at first.

Everyone is capable of visualising. Just imagine right now the colour and any design features of the curtains or blinds that hang in your bedroom window (or any other window for that matter). Imagine the face of a friend. You can do it. Different people will do so with varying levels of clarity and everyone can do it.

Imagine that you have a remote control for your mind – you can play around with making pictures clearer or bigger or brighter or you can step in and out of the pictures – enjoy playing!

We invite you to experiment and to simply notice how you best imagine future situations most powerfully and realistically so that you are fully connected into the experience of it (associated) and have a sense that you are already living it. That is when the positive programming of a goal into your system is most effective.

Imagining progress towards your goal and successful completion of your goal in pictures or movies on that inner screen (your minds eye) is a great way for many people to bring the scenario alive. For others it may be that imagining hearing the sounds present whilst achieving your goal is the most powerful starting point, or giving a powerful narration of what is happening (in present tense language) or feeling the feelings (of any movement, sense of touch, temperature etc and also any inner feelings that we tend to call emotions).

Use your powerful imagination to combine a whole range of powerful sensory experiences as you enjoy 'living' your success journey up front in your mind!

Experiment with accessing the smells and tastes too! It all makes the programming even more compelling!

The exact way that you represent your positive future so that it seems like you are already living it will be a personal approach that is unique to you.

So enjoy experimenting and go with the flow of however the positive mental representations come to you most powerfully.

Some people like to set hours aside each day to do such mental rehearsal and equally many people decide to start the day and end the day with a few minutes of priming their system for success through mental rehearsal. Still other people snatch every opportunity to spend a few moments to top up the programming – for example you could mentally rehearse as you get a shower in the morning and then as you travel to work (or wherever you are travelling to) you could be narrating a powerful description of your future unfolding (either out loud or in your head – with tonality). You might choose to write a few lines about the live experience of achieving your goal whilst waiting for something to download to your computer or whilst waiting for a kettle to boil (or whatever else).

Everyone can make time for mental rehearsal in one form or another and I ask you to consider how important it is for you to step up and achieve your goals. If it *is* important to you, then make it a priority to mentally rehearse regularly!

Exercise

Allow yourself to imagine successfully achieving the outcome(s) that you decided upon in step 1. You can do this by filling your mind with internal movies of the whole experience you want to have. Give yourself a remote control changing the finer details of the pictures, the sounds, the feelings, and any other information that is useful to notice. Play the movies that give you the best feelings over and over again and enjoy! Also weave into the experiences that you are rehearsing all of the evidence that you have captured in step 4 (the debate) that support the possibilities you raised in step 3 (what-iffing).

Be playful with this process – enjoy rehearsing your success, knowing that by doing so you are helping to skew the odds in your favour!

Chapter 9

Step 6 in our 6-Step
Belief Change Process:
Step into an empowered
role, ready for action

Having completed steps 4 and 5, your whole system will now thoroughly believe the positive alternative to the unhelpful old belief (that you noticed in step 2).

The old belief is now outdated and your system will enjoy accepting the new position as 'truth'.

Step 6, the final step in the process, is about getting out there armed with your new truth and taking the actions that will allow you to attract and experience the next wave of evidence to further support the fact that this new belief is totally true for you.

To get out there to take appropriate action most effectively, we are going to ask you to access and step into your most empowered roles.

So often, people will raise the bar on their performance and shine fully when they step into particular roles. We have all heard of those extraordinary stories when an old lady has found themselves in the position of playing the role of life saver and has ended up performing an outstanding feat like ripping a car door open to get to and rescue her grandchildren!

The role we assign ourselves consciously or unconsciously in any moment has a massive effect on the resources we access and what we ultimately achieve. Often when we are being a role model to someone (for example as a parent, boss, supportive friend, trainer or demonstrator of excellent practice) it brings out the absolute best in us. The gates open on our inner resources and we shine. We perform. We get results.

The great news is that we can step into an empowering role at any time, simply by imagining having the right people with us so we can assign ourselves the role of role model and go about being an example of excellence for them.

We have tested this thoroughly in lots of different contexts with many, many people and it works an absolute treat!

Let me give you an example to illustrate…

First I will tell you about a woman that I had observed many times showing a full-on fear response in the presence of wasps. She could be seen running around screaming and waving her hands in the air and flicking her hair about as she went (interestingly the very behaviours likely to increase the likelihood of being stung by a wasp).

Then on one occasion I happened to be in a position to see her show a very different response to a wasp flying near to her.

I saw her walking *towards* the wasp. This was a first!

She was reassuring others around her saying 'It is only a wasp' in a calm voice. Armed only with a small piece of flimsy paper she gently wafted the wasp out of the window and went back to what she was doing a few moments before.

Wow! A completely different response than I had ever seen in her before when faced by a wasp and yet it seemed so very effortless and natural.

So what was going on?

Well in this particular scenario, she was in the role of teacher in front of a class of 30+ young students and she had realised that she was a role model to these children and that her actions were going to be potentially influential on the individuals in her care.

So she stepped up. She raised the bar! And in doing so, she opened the gates on her inner resources and dealt with it calmly and effectively! Result!

I spoke with her afterwards and she admitted that although there was a certain amount of 'putting on a brave face' she was also very genuinely feeling a lot more resourceful than when she was in other situations (such as the times I had seen her in the staffroom or at events outside of the school situation). Not only that, the act of stepping up in her empowering role as a role model allowed her to generate genuine experiential evidence that she could successfully deal with things and that 'nothing bad happened'. Her system would remember that! And of course the more she could repeat that empowered experience, the more embedded would become any belief that it was possible for her to deal with wasps safely and effectively.

So how did she take things forward?

Well we agreed that a great strategy for her whenever she encountered a wasp would be to immediately bring to mind being in the role of teacher and to imagine her students being there with her, ready to be influenced by her responses.

It worked!

From that point on, whenever she noticed a wasp she just stepped into her role model role and dealt with it all very calmly. Simple, yet very effective!

In fact so much so that after only a few repetitions, every cell in her system *knew* that it was safe to deal with wasps in that way and she *knew* at every level that she was more than a match to this kind of situation.

The best news is that she generalised this principle to other areas of her life where she had previously held unhelpful beliefs and done fear or anxiety responses. She began to experiment with converting other types of unhelpful responses into more helpful ones by stepping into empowering roles.

Another compelling demonstration of the power of stepping into an empowering role relates to the activity of making sales calls.

Lots of people can relate to having felt anxious about making sales calls and for a particular client of mine, the anxiety had been so strong that he had avoided making the calls altogether.

His business was suffering. He needed more leads!

I knew (from his other interests) that there were many areas in life where he was already showing much confidence and where he was being a positive role model to others. He liked to help people and he liked to set a positive example and I sensed that this could be harnessed to help him to access his confidence around sales calls.

I asked him to imagine that a work experience student had arrived in his company, eager to learn and looking to him for an example of how to make confident sales calls. I asked him what he would do in such a situation!

After a moment of accessing the imagined scene, he said slowly and clearly… 'You know what, I'd just get on and do it! And as a matter of fact, I also reckon I'd do it well and do it confidently'.

This flagged up to him immediately that he already had the *capacity* to make sales calls confidently; it was just that he needed the right triggers to be able to access that confidence.

So I had him visualising that very situation – and also had him imagine that there was a camera set up in his office, ready to automatically start filming whenever he was making sales calls, so it could capture effective and confident calls for the benefit of the student on work experience.

Now, of course he knew very well that this was just a mental trick. And it was a mental trick that worked. So we used it!

It made all the difference. He just stepped up, raised the bar, opened the gates on his inner resources and performed! And performed well! And of course he very quickly got the evidence that he could do it, he could survive it and that actually it was a very safe and even at times an enjoyable and satisfying activity.

We helped a professional business trainer who was going to have a meeting with an important customer who was angry about an aspect of delivery from one of his team. He was at first daunted about the idea of going into that meeting. He had already spoken with the customer on the phone and had detected a lot of anger and frustration.

We asked him what he would do if he was in his trainer role and he was demonstrating to his delegates how to effectively and calmly handle a situation with an angry and frustrated customer. He thought for a moment and then quickly said that he would handle it confidently and effectively.

So we asked him to first of all to mentally rehearse operating in that trainer role and then on the day of the meeting he was to step into that role. He was asked to assume as he walked into the customer's office that he was indeed training people to handle such challenging meetings well and that they would be observing his performance to learn some useful positive lessons.

And he did it!

He reported back that he had performed well. He left the customer feeling good and as a side effect he reinforced his own beliefs that he was indeed capable of handling even tough situations in his business (and his life).

On a personal note, we regularly take imaginary friends out with us when we are coaching, training or delivering keynote speeches. Imagining having trainee coaches, or less experienced trainers and speakers with us, people who are learning from our every word and action, will inevitably raise our bar and enables us to open the gates on our resources, helping us to really shine and perform.

Also we (and many people we have worked with) have found that accessing the role of responsible and caring parent works really well – imagining showing our child how to confidently and competently handle situations tends to help us to really pull that extra resourcefulness into play.

Exercise:

Consider:

Who would you be being a role model to in order to raise the bar on your performance?

Who would you need to imagine being there with you for you to open the gates on your resources to achieve your desired outcomes and goals?

We encourage you to start to experiment with this in your imagination and do whatever works to become really practised at stepping into being the best role model that you can be!

Chapter 10

Dipping in, sharing
and stepping up:
Onwards and upwards!

When all six steps have been applied wholeheartedly to making those important belief shifts, you will have freed yourself to thrive.

You will also recognise that this whole process can be generalised to change any belief about anything or anyone at any time when you notice that a current belief is 'getting in the way'.

We encourage you to do just that!

Each of the steps is powerful in its own right and so please do experiment with dipping in to any of the steps in isolation, as sometimes just doing one of these activities is enough to create a major shift in perception and belief and then performance.

One of the ways that we would encourage you to help yourself to ingrain these principles and practices at a deeper level so that it becomes second nature to you is to help others with the approaches you have learned.

Share the six steps with people when they are inviting support to make an important change.

Help others to understand that a belief is just a belief and that it can be helpful or unhelpful and if it is unhelpful it can be changed for good. This will be a gift that can help them to step up in life and by the very giving of that gift you will be stepping up higher too!

Remember, beliefs are, in effect, gatekeepers on a person's potential. They can open up the person's resource gates wide so they shine brightly and achieve what they deserve to achieve or they can slam those resource gates shut so that only an impoverished version of the person is shining through into experience and performance.

You can imagine the difference between showing up each day shining at 100% resourcefulness compared to turning up with only a fraction of that resourcefulness ready to be expressed.

Everything changes when we show up as the best version of ourselves shining through at 100%.

You perform better, you enjoy life better, life is easier, your direction is clear, you make more of a difference out there and you feel fulfilled.

By taking control of your own beliefs you metaphorically leap over from the passenger seat to the driving seat of your own life.

Many people are living well short of their potential because they have not yet made that important leap. Make sure that you and the people that you love, support and care about (and any complete strangers that you feel compelled to support) take the opportunity to live life at its fullest by harnessing the simple yet powerful tools contained within this book. Pass your copy of this book onto others (or buy them a copy) and send a positive ripple out into the universe because you never know how far reaching that positive ripple might be.

A belief that has always served me very well since I adopted it is that 'When I send positive ripples out into the world, my positive return will be at least a thousand times greater and that positive return will begin immediately with a good feeling inside'. Try that belief on for yourself and if it works for you – adopt it! And if you prefer a different one, create the perfect one for you and then use the 6 steps to reinforce it!

Give yourself full permission to thoroughly enjoy harnessing the power of your beliefs for good and we would love to hear your success stories as they unfold.

Please email us about your successes at: info@aha-success.com

Embrace every day with gratitude that you have another opportunity to live life to the full and enjoy being magnificent YOU!

Appendix

French-Burgess Belief
Gates Model of Human
Experience & Performance

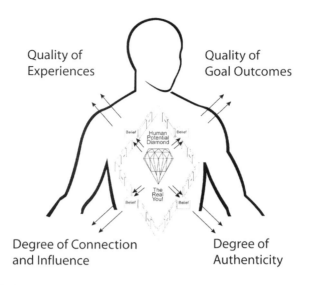

Quality of Experiences

Quality of Goal Outcomes

Degree of Connection and Influence

Degree of Authenticity

The model above has been designed to illustrate how a person's beliefs can allow them to experience and express their full potential or get in the way of this happening. We believe (and it is a belief that has served us well as change-facilitators) that human beings come into the world with magnificent potential (represented by the human potential diamond in the model) and that this potential flows freely in a new born baby and is mainly applied to 'being in the moment', focusing on securing what is needed for survival and learning about their environment and the people in that environment.

As this 'learning' happens over the coming weeks, months, years and decades the person has 'lessons' that come from observing others, from listening to others, from direct experience of interacting with the environment and from taking on the cultural rules that they are being surrounded by.

These 'learning' experiences start to put some 'conditions' upon the person freely expressing and living their full potential and these conditions are captured in the beliefs that the person develops as they learn. We have represented this in the model by the development of 'belief gates' (which we also refer to as 'resource gates' because the person's beliefs affect how much of their true potential and resourcefulness shines through moment by moment).

Some of the person's learning experiences lead to the formation of beliefs that allow 'belief gates' (or 'resource gates') to remain wide open so the person's magnificent potential and resourcefulness continues to shine through easily in the contexts where those beliefs are active.

Some other learning experiences lead to the formation of beliefs that shut off some of the person's magnificent potential and resourcefulness, in particular contexts where those beliefs are active (in other words, some of the 'belief gates' or the 'resource gates' close on the potential).

The extent to which a person's magnificent potential 'shines' through and positively affects results will depend upon how many and to what extent 'belief gates' are open or closed. A closed 'belief gate' represents that a belief is 'getting in the way' of a person attaining their desired outcomes and a fully open 'belief gate' represents that a belief is 'smoothing the way' to a person attaining their desired outcomes. A belief gate can of course be partially open and the degree to which a gate is open may vary from context to context.

The task of any individual on their personal development journey to stepping up in their life is to get those belief gates open wide in as many useful contexts as possible.

The task of any change-facilitator is to be a catalyst for gate opening,

The best news conveyed by this model is that the deepest truth is that the magnificent potential of the person is permanent. The diamond is always shining! If the person is not experiencing it so or the person's performance is not suggesting it is so then all it means is that some belief gates (or resource gates) have 'got in the way' of the shining potential getting through. The gate closure is temporary – any closed gate can be opened again (no matter how long it appears to have been shut).

A really powerful way to get 'belief gates' open again to allow someone to reconnect with their magnificent potential (in experience and performance) is to apply the 'French-Burgess 6 step belief change process' to key belief(s) that have been keeping the gate(s) closed.

About the authors

Tony Burgess is a Director of the
Academy of High Achievers
www.aha-success.com

As an experienced trainer, facilitator, speaker,
firewalk instructor and coach, most of Tony's
time is now spent designing, co-coordinating and
delivering performance-enhancing and life-enriching
programmes for people who are hungry for more
success and fulfilment in their lives.

Tony has worked with business leaders, teams within organisations,
entrepreneurs, educators, students, performers, sports people and
members of the public to help them to tap into and release the full
potential of their personal resources, preparing them to attain whatever
outcomes they set out to achieve and much more besides.

Tony has a degree in psychology, and for the last 14 years he has
specialised in helping people to thrive in their endeavours by teaching
them powerful mental fitness techniques and offering them super-effective
connection and communication tools.

Tony is a specialist in utilising a powerful blend of applied psychology
and he often draws on his expertise in the areas of NLP and DiSC® in his
presentations.

Tony's core philosophy is based on living his truth and by congruent
example he constantly strives to inspire others to shine brighter.

Contact Tony at tburgess@aha-success.com

Julie French is a Director of the Academy of High Achievers www.aha-success.com

Building on a successful earlier career as a senior manager leading large teams, managing multi-million-pound budgets and operating at board level, Julie now works with companies and organisations that are going through change and need to improve their internal relationships. Her specific expertise is in people management, handling conflict and effective communication.

Julie is an outstanding executive coach, master practitioner and certified trainer in Neuro Linguistic Programming (NLP), a certified trainer

in 'Everything DiSC®' and is also a certified professional speaker and firewalk instructor. Combining exceptional listening skills with a creative and empowering approach, Julie assists organisations and individuals to realise their vision.

Julie loves life and one of her great characteristics is in 'exploding warmth' wherever she goes!

Contact Julie at jfrench@aha-success.com

Together

Tony and Julie deliver on stage seamlessly. As partners in business and in life, day by day they are living and breathing their passion for helping people achieve at the highest level and it adds a whole different dimension to a keynote (or conference or workshop) to have the two of them enthusiastically and professionally delivering together in such a natural and free-flowing way. In terms of connection with an audience, the male–female combination on stage helps ensure that the message gets through easily and effectively to all who are watching and listening.

Train to become a practitioner in belief change work

This book already provides you with the tools to start immediately working on aligning your own beliefs with your desired outcomes and also to significantly help others to make positive shifts too.

And if you should choose to, you can now gain direct access to our training to become a practitioner in our 'Belief Gates Personal Empowerment System'.

This unique training programme brings alive the full teachings contained within this book plus practical demonstration and direct experience of the concepts and tools in practice.

Participating will help you to tap into the power of the French-Burgess Belief Gates Model of human performance and experience (see appendix, page 76) and also to gain valuable experience in using our 6-step belief change process, enabling you to take your performance in change work to a whole new level.

Your trainers and facilitators for this unique training are us – Tony Burgess and Julie French.

We would love to meet you, welcome you and work with you to help you to make a massive positive difference in the world!

For more information about our practitioner training in our 'Belief Gates Personal Empowerment System' please visit the appropriate page on our website:

http://www.aha-success.com/beliefgates.html